A DAY IN THE LIFE OF A
PHARAOH

Emma Helbrough

Illustrated by Inklink, Firenze

PowerKiDS
press.
New York

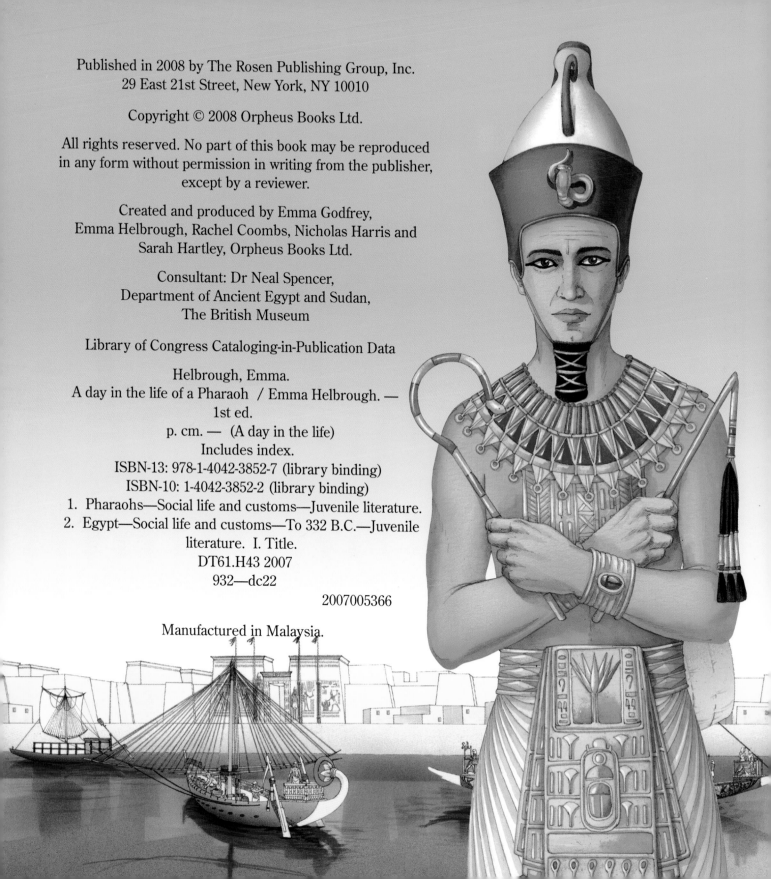

Published in 2008 by The Rosen Publishing Group, Inc.
29 East 21st Street, New York, NY 10010

Created and produced by Emma Godfrey,
Emma Helbrough, Rachel Coombs, Nicholas Harris and
Sarah Hartley, Orpheus Books Ltd.

Consultant: Dr Neal Spencer,
Department of Ancient Egypt and Sudan,
The British Museum

Library of Congress Cataloging-in-Publication Data

Helbrough, Emma.
A day in the life of a Pharaoh / Emma Helbrough. —
1st ed.
p. cm. — (A day in the life)
Includes index.
ISBN-13: 978-1-4042-3852-7 (library binding)
ISBN-10: 1-4042-3852-2 (library binding)
1. Pharaohs—Social life and customs—Juvenile literature.
2. Egypt—Social life and customs—To 332 B.C.—Juvenile
literature. I. Title.
DT61.H43 2007
932—dc22
                                         2007005366

Manufactured in Malaysia.

CONTENTS

ABOUT THIS BOOK

I n this fascinating book you will follow a very busy day in the life of a pharaoh in ancient Egypt. Along the way, you will learn all about what life was like for a pharaoh, from his royal duties to the food he ate and the games he played.

MAKING OFFERINGS

A fter a breakfast of bread and fruit, Ramesses visits the temple of Karnak to wake the god Amun-Ra who lives there. With the help of two priests, Ramesses follows the daily ritual, washing the statue, presenting it with new clothes, making offerings of fresh fruit, sacred lotus flowers and wine, and then bowing down to pray before it.

As Egypt's high priest, it is very important that Ramesses fulfills this important duty. If he were to ignore it, he would risk angering Amun-Ra, king of all gods, who might bring terrible luck upon Egypt.

Pharaoh's wisdom

Roughly how many gods did the Egyptians worship?

a) Ten
b) One hundred
c) One thousand

Look out for these questions. Answers are on page 31.

This is Pharaoh Ramesses. He is the main character in this story.

TELLING THE TIME

There is a clock in the corner of each page, so you can check what time it is in the story, but in truth the ancient Egyptians did not use mechanical clocks like this one to tell the time, as they had not been invented yet.

Many people used water clocks. A water clock is a bowl filled with water. The water slowly drains out of a hole near the bottom of the bowl. The time is told by checking the water level off against markings on the inside of the bowl. Water clocks had one big disadvantage, however. They had to be refilled each time the water ran out.

These illustrations show how a water clock works. As the water drains away, time markers are revealed.

4

ANCIENT EGYPT

Ancient Egyptian civilization began to thrive along the banks of the Nile River in North Africa over 5,000 years ago and remained powerful for over 3,500 years. This story is set roughly 3,300 years ago, around the year 1270 B.C.

Egypt at that time was a land of contrasts. The rich people, including our pharaoh, lived very comfortable lives, with servants and slaves to look after them. They ate well and lived in large homes. However, most people were poor peasants. They worked hard farming the lands and building temples and tombs for the rich. Many ancient Egyptian buildings still stand today. The most famous are the pyramids, which were built to house the remains of early Egyptian pharaohs.

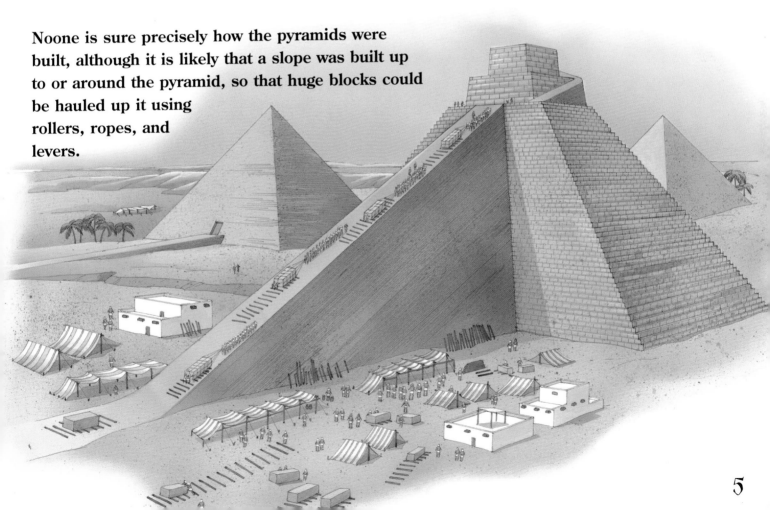

Noone is sure precisely how the pyramids were built, although it is likely that a slope was built up to or around the pyramid, so that huge blocks could be hauled up it using rollers, ropes, and levers.

GETTING DRESSED

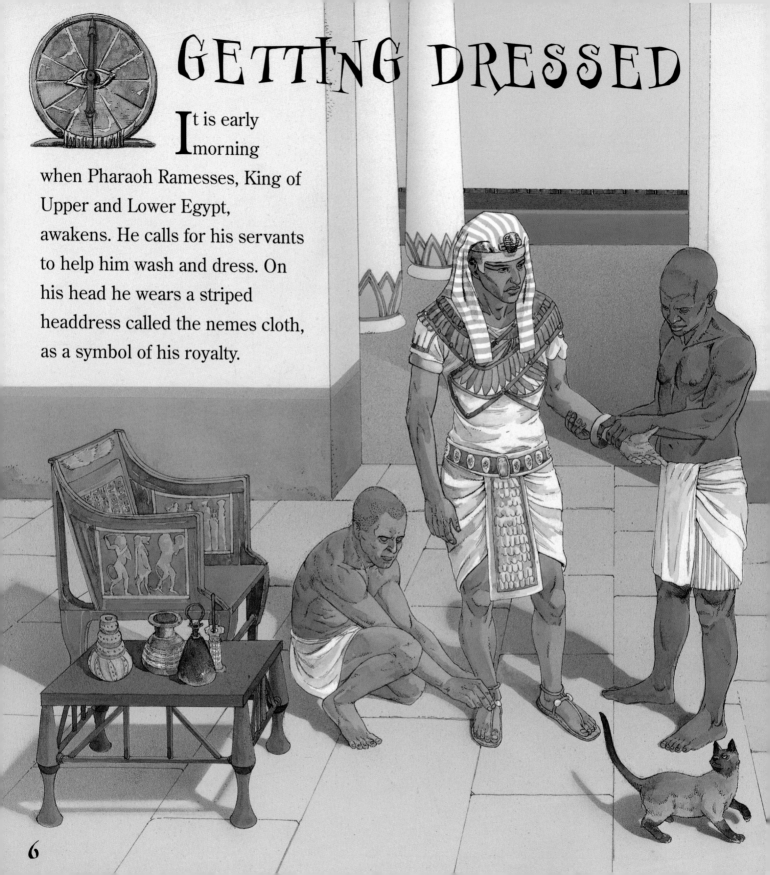

It is early morning when Pharaoh Ramesses, King of Upper and Lower Egypt, awakens. He calls for his servants to help him wash and dress. On his head he wears a striped headdress called the nemes cloth, as a symbol of his royalty.

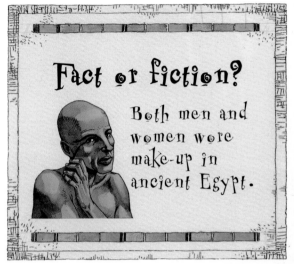

A golden cobra on his forehead represents the goddess Wadjet, protector of Egypt. His eyes are made up with thick black lines and he has a long, false beard fixed to his chin.

Today is the start of the annual Opet festival. There will be much celebrating throughout Egypt, but before then, Ramesses has many royal duties to attend to. First of all there will be a meeting with his vizier, or chief advisor, who will inform him of any important political matters.

MAKING OFFERINGS

After a breakfast of bread and fruit, Ramesses visits the temple of Karnak to wake the god Amun-Ra who lives there. With the help of two priests, Ramesses follows the daily ritual, washing the statue, presenting it with new clothes, making offerings of fresh fruit, sacred lotus flowers and wine, and then bowing down to pray before it.

As Egypt's high priest, it is very important that Ramesses fulfills this important duty. If he were to ignore it, he would risk angering Amun-Ra, king of all gods, who might bring terrible luck upon Egypt.

Pharaoh's wisdom

Roughly how many gods did the Egyptians worship?

a) Ten
b) One hundred
c) One thousand

9

JUDGING

It is now ten o'clock, and Ramesses and his vizier are seated in the temple listening to a court case. Two men kneel before him, begging forgiveness for their crimes. Scribes take notes as the vizier recounts how the men were caught stealing from a dead pharaoh's tomb. This angers Ramesses. He cannot understand how anyone could have so little respect for the dead. This calls for a very serious punishment.

Fact or fiction?

Ancient Egyptians wrote in hieroglyphs.

VISITORS

By late morning, a long line
of ambassadors from the
countries surrounding Egypt
has arrived. Each ambassador
brings lavish gifts to present to Ramesses, from
gold vessels to beautiful rugs and clothes. These gifts
are meant as a sign of respect, acknowledging that Egypt conquered
their lands many years ago.

Two ambassadors from Syria have brought a very unusual gift: a
large brown bear, which stands on its hind legs before him.
Ramesses is delighted with the bear, which he will put in his zoo.

13

Fact or fiction?

Pharaohs were mummified because they believed they would need their bodies for the next life.

At one o'clock Ramesses leaves the temple and is carried on a platform to the banks of the Nile River, which flows through the heart of Egypt on its way to the Mediterranean Sea.

As always, the river is busy with traffic. There are large boats carrying great statues to nearby temples and small boats carrying people to or from work. Everyone in Egypt travels by boat, as it is the fastest and most convenient way to get around.

Ramesses and his entourage board the royal vessel, and soon they set sail. The pharaoh is on his way to visit his unfinished tomb. Ramesses makes regular trips there to see how the work is progressing. Like every pharaoh, he wants his tomb to be just right, as he will be spending eternity there after his death.

ON THE NILE

Further down the Nile, the boat sails past farmlands on the river banks. Ramesses watches his people harvesting the last of this season's crops. Soon the lush, green banks will flood with water.

16

When the floods die down and the water drains away, leaving the land damp and fertile, new crops will be planted and the whole cycle can begin again.

Ramesses recoils at the sight of a crocodile as it drifts by. Everyone stays well away from crocodiles, as they would make a meal of you given the chance!

Fact or fiction?

Pharaohs were always buried inside pyramids.

HUNTING

The last leg of the journey to the tomb crosses the dry, dusty desert. This gives Ramesses an opportunity to take part in his favorite sport: lion hunting. Lions are fast and ferocious, and provide a real challenge even for a highly skilled hunter like the pharaoh. He soons finds a pair and the chase begins.

The chariot clatters over the stony ground with sand spraying out behind it. The pharaoh's pack of hunting dogs bark and yelp as they close in on the lions. A servant takes the horses' reins while Ramesses tries hard to steady his aim with his bow and arrow. The lions are moving quickly and he may only get one clear shot at them.

A ROYAL VISIT

At about three o'clock, Ramesses reaches the tomb workers' village. This is where all the craftsmen and laborers live with their families. It is very isolated from the rest of Egypt as no-one else would want to live in the barren desert. As the pharaoh makes his way through the village streets, carried on a raised platform, the villagers come out to greet him. Many bow down as he passes by. He is treated with enormous respect by all, as to them he is both a ruler and a protector.

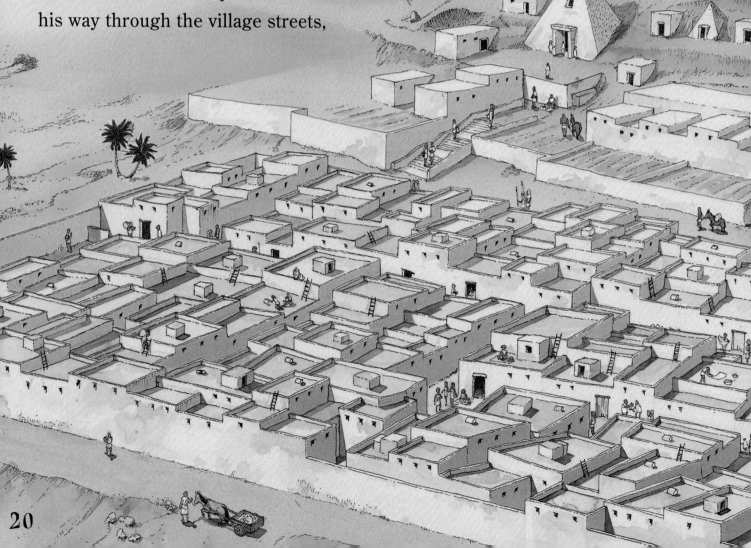

Pharaoh's wisdom

Roughly how many years did it take to build a pyramid?

a) Five
b) Twenty
c) Fifty

As Ramesses passes through the village, he glances inside the workmen's homes. They are very far removed from his lavish palace. Their tiny, high windows allow only a little light in, but, more importantly, keep the sun's hot rays out. He also notices the small shrines at the back of each house, where his people pray to the gods each day.

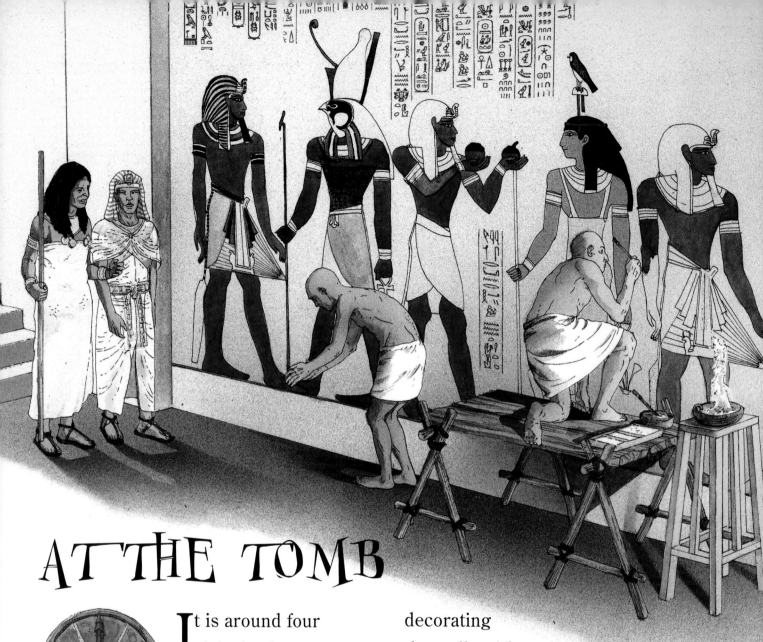

AT THE TOMB

It is around four o'clock when Ramesses enters his his future tomb, accompanied by his vizier. Inside, the pharaoh is pleased to find that work is progressing well. Sculptors and painters are now decorating the walls with drawings and hieroglyphs which tell stories of the pharaoh's life. Working by torchlight alone, the sculptors first carve drawings into the tomb walls. Then the painters bring the scenes to life with color.

One artist is grinding up natural minerals, dug up from the earth, to make the different color paints. He is mixing up warm reds, yellows and oranges, and even bright blues and greens. The artists use lots of black paint, too, to create the thick black outlines. For this they use a paint made from charcoal.

Ramesses watches the craftsmen hard at work for some time, before deciding it is time to return home.

Pharaoh's wisdom

What did a pharaoh have buried with him?

a) His jewelry
b) His furniture
c) His pets

23

RIVER SPORT

On his way back to the city of Thebes, Ramesses decides he would like to do some more hunting. This time he hunts waterfowl nesting in the reeds which grow along the banks of the Nile.

He glides silently through the water in a small boat made from papyrus reeds, paddled by a servant. His pet cat sits at the front, watching the birds intently and startling them into flight.

As the birds flutter away, Ramesses hurtles his throwing stick at one, and the bird drops into the water. His cat licks its lips in anticipation, as they paddle over to collect the dead bird.

The birds' commotion has disturbed a hippopotamus wading in the water. It rears its head angrily and bares its teeth at them. Ramesses's servant paddles away furiously, knowing that it is very unwise to upset a hippopotamus!

OPET FESTIVAL

Back at Thebes, the sun is beginning to set as Ramesses leads the Opet festival procession. He is carried in a sacred boat called a barque from the banks of the Nile along sphinx-lined avenues to the steps of the temple of Karnak. The pharaoh is followed by acrobats, singers, and dancers scattering flower petals.

Fact or fiction?

Many temples and tombs were buried under sand for thousands of years.

TIME TO RELAX

It is now eight o'clock, and Ramesses has at last returned home to his palace. The evening is a rare time for relaxation, and the pharaoh is playing a board game called senet with his son. Although the sun has set, it is still very warm, so a servant wafts a fan gently above their heads.

The pharaoh's pet lion, Tiy, prowls the room, growling at anyone who dares look him in the eye. Ramesses keeps the lion both as a symbol of his great power and to intimidate his enemies.

Entertainers dance and sway to the sound of a harp. The harpist sings a popular song which tells people to make the most of their time on Earth because life is just a dream. Ramesses tries hard to concentrate on the words, but the melody makes him feel sleepy. After all, it has been a very busy day.

Pharaoh's wisdom

Which of these materials was expensive in ancient Egypt? Can you think why?

a) Wood
b) Glass
c) Pottery

(Hint: Egypt was mainly desert)

29

GLOSSARY

Here you can check the meaning of some of the words in this book.

ambassador (am-BA-suh-der) Somebody who visits another country as a representative of their own country.

chariot (CHER-ee-ut) A small cart drawn by horses, often used in sport and warfare.

hieroglyphs (HY-uh-ruh-glifs) A method of writing with pictures.

mummy (MUH-mee) A body that has been preserved after death and then wrapped in cloth.

offering (O-fuh-ring) A gift offered to a god to show respect.

opet festival (OP-et FES-tuh-vul) An ancient Egyptian festival which was held once a year.

papyrus (puh-PY-rus) A reed that grows along river banks and can be used to make papyrus paper and boats.

pharaoh (FER-oh) The king, high priest, and ruler of ancient Egypt.

pyramid (PIR-uh-mid) A pharaoh's tomb with four sloping triangular sides.

scribe (SKRYB) A person trained to read and write in ancient Egypt.

senet (SEN-et) A board game popular in ancient Egyptian times.

shrine (SHRYN) A place where people go to worship a god.

sphinx (SFINGKS) A statue in the shape of a lion with a human or ram's head.

statue (STA-choo) A sculpture representing a god, human, or animal.

tomb (TOOM) A building or underground vault where a person is buried.

vizier (vuh-ZIR) The person responsible for the day-to-day running of Egypt.

ANSWERS

Page 7 – Fact! In ancient Egypt it was fashionable for everyone to wear make-up. People didn't realize, though, that the lead-based paints they were using were actually poisonous.

Page 8 – c. The ancient Egyptians worshipped about a thousand different gods and goddesses altogether, although some fell in and out of favor. They built temples for their gods to live inside.

Page 10 – Fact! Hieroglyphs were a way of writing with pictures. Most ancient Egyptians could not write, but specially trained people called scribes decorated the walls of tombs and temples with hieroglyphs.

Page 14 – Fact! Ancient Egyptians believed that when a pharaoh died, he would go on living just as he did on Earth, which is why the Egyptians tried to preserve their pharaohs' bodies after death. They rubbed them with oils and wrapped them in linen bandages.

Page 17 – Fiction! Early Egyptian pharaohs were buried in pyramids, but these were often robbed because they were easy to find. Later pharaohs, such as the one in this story, were buried in hidden underground tombs.

Page 21 – b. It took about twenty years to build a pyramid or tomb. As soon as a new pharaoh took the throne, he began the preparations for building his tomb.

Page 23 – All of them! Pharaohs had all kinds of worldly possessions buried with them, from gold vessels to furniture and pets.

Page 27 – Fact! Many Egyptian tombs remained buried for thousands of years. There may be others that are still hidden.

Page 29 – a. Wood was very expensive in ancient Egyptian times because hardly any trees grew in the desert. Wood had to be shipped in from far away and so it was reserved for the rich.

INDEX